TRAGEDY! TALES FROM THE TITANIC

Haunted Titanic Stories

BY SARAH EASON

ILLUSTRATED BY ALBERTO SAICHANN

BEARPORT PUBLISHING

Minneapolis, Minnesota

BEAR CLAW

Credits

20, © Shutterstock/Meunierd; 21t, © Alamy/Peter Muhly; 21r, © Shutterstock/EML; 22t, © Wikimedia Commons; 22b, © Wikimedia Commons/Beyond My Ken; 23, © Alamy/Lee Brown.

Editor: Jennifer Sanderson
Proofreader: Katie Dicker
Designer: Paul Myerscough
Picture Researcher: Katie Dicker

Bearport Publishing Company Product Development Team

Publisher: Jen Jenson; Director of Product Development: Spencer Brinker; Managing Editor: Allison Juda; Editor: Cole Nelson; Associate Editor: Naomi Reich; Associate Editor: Tiana Tran; Art Director: Colin O'Dea; Designer: Kim Jones; Designer: Kayla Eggert; Product Development Specialist: Owen Hamlin

Statement on Usage of Generative Artificial Intelligence

Bearport Publishing remains committed to publishing high-quality nonfiction books. Therefore, we restrict the use of generative AI to ensure accuracy of all text and visual components pertaining to a book's subject. See BearportPublishing.com for details.

A Note on Graphic Narrative Nonfiction

This graphic story is a dramatization based on true events. It is intended to give the reader a sense of the narrative rather than a presentation of actual details as they occurred.

Library of Congress Cataloging-in-Publication Data

Names: Eason, Sarah, author. | Saichann, Alberto, illustrator.
Title: Haunted Titanic stories / Sarah Eason ; Illustrated by Alberto
  Saichann.
Description: Bear claw books. | Minneapolis, Minnesota : Bearport
  Publishing Company, 2025. | Series: Tragedy! tales from the titanic |
  Includes bibliographical references and index.
Identifiers: LCCN 2024035014 (print) | LCCN 2024035015 (ebook) | ISBN
  9798892328593 (library binding) | ISBN 9798892329491 (paperback) | ISBN
  9798892328661 (ebook)
Subjects: LCSH: Titanic (Steamship)--Juvenile literature. | Titanic
  (Steamship)--Comic books, strips, etc. | Haunted ships--Great
  Britain--History--20th century--Juvenile literature. | Haunted
  ships--Great Britain--History--20th century--Comic books, strips, etc. |
  Ocean liners--Great Britain--History--20th century--Juvenile literature.
  | Ocean liners--Great Britain--History--20th century--Comic books,
  strips, etc. | Shipwrecks--North Atlantic Ocean--History--20th
  century--Juvenile literature. | Shipwrecks--North Atlantic
  Ocean--History--20th century--Comic books, strips, etc. | Graphic
  novels.
Classification: LCC G530.T6 E28 2025 (print) | LCC G530.T6 (ebook) | DDC
  910.9163/4--dc23/eng20240731
LC record available at https://lccn.loc.gov/2024035014
LC ebook record available at https://lccn.loc.gov/2024035015

For more information, write to Bearport Publishing, 5357 Penn Avenue South, Minneapolis, MN 55419.

Contents

CHAPTER I

Southampton's Sadness

Frankie Ford had always loved big ships. Ever since she was a child in Southampton, England, she enjoyed watching huge **ocean liners** glide across the skyline from her bedroom window.

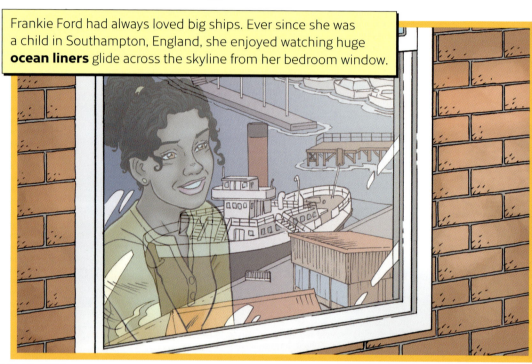

She shared this passion with her grandmother. Sometimes, they would sit and watch the ships together.

WOW! LOOK AT THAT ONE!

INCREDIBLE! IT MUST BE ONE OF THE BIGGEST IN THE WORLD. IT REMINDS ME OF WHAT MY GRAN TOLD ME ABOUT *TITANIC*.

TITANIC! DID YOUR GRANDMA SEE THE *TITANIC*?

SEE IT? SHE WAVED IT OFF!

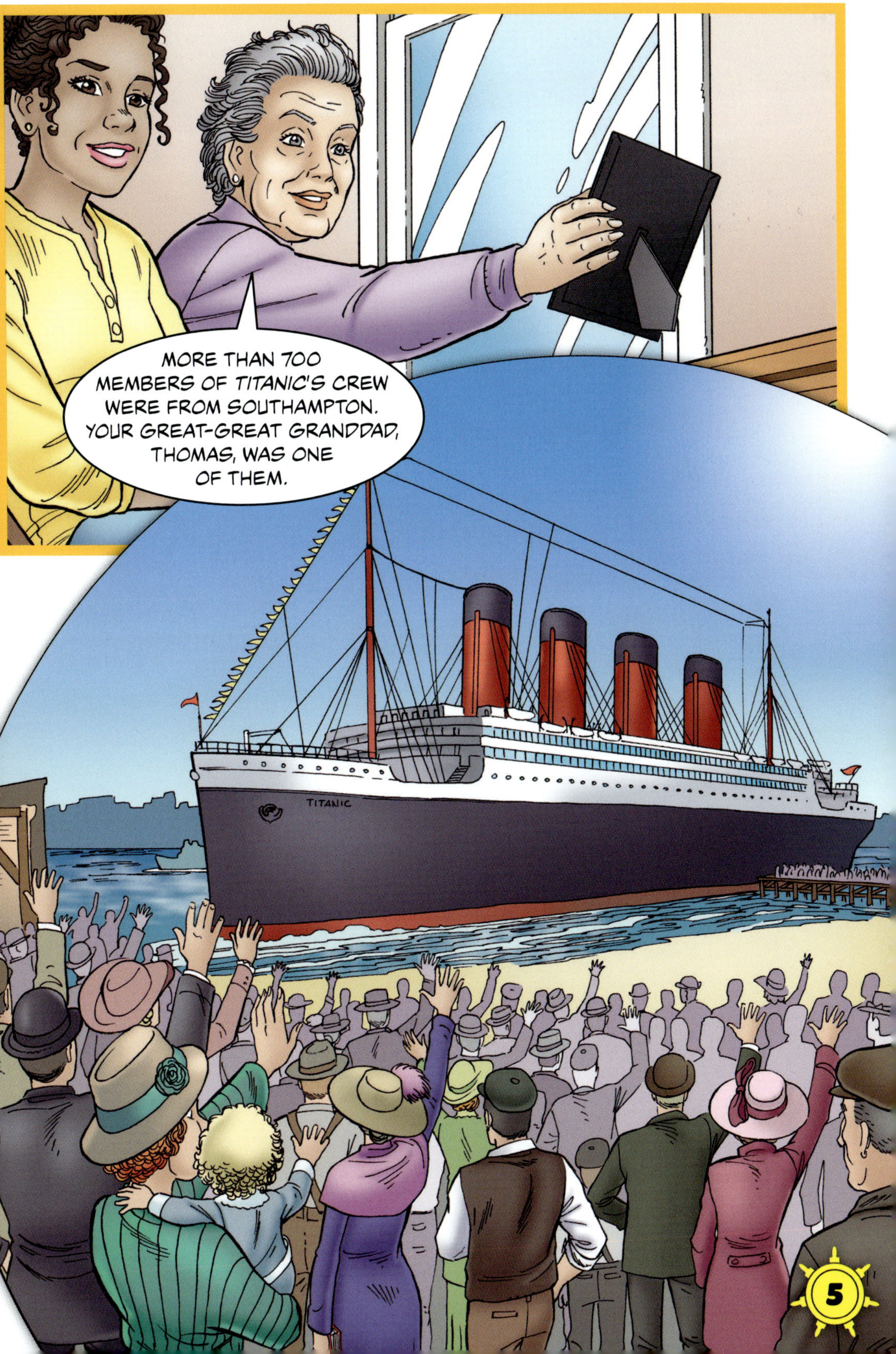
MORE THAN 700 MEMBERS OF *TITANIC'S* CREW WERE FROM SOUTHAMPTON. YOUR GREAT-GREAT GRANDDAD, THOMAS, WAS ONE OF THEM.
TITANIC

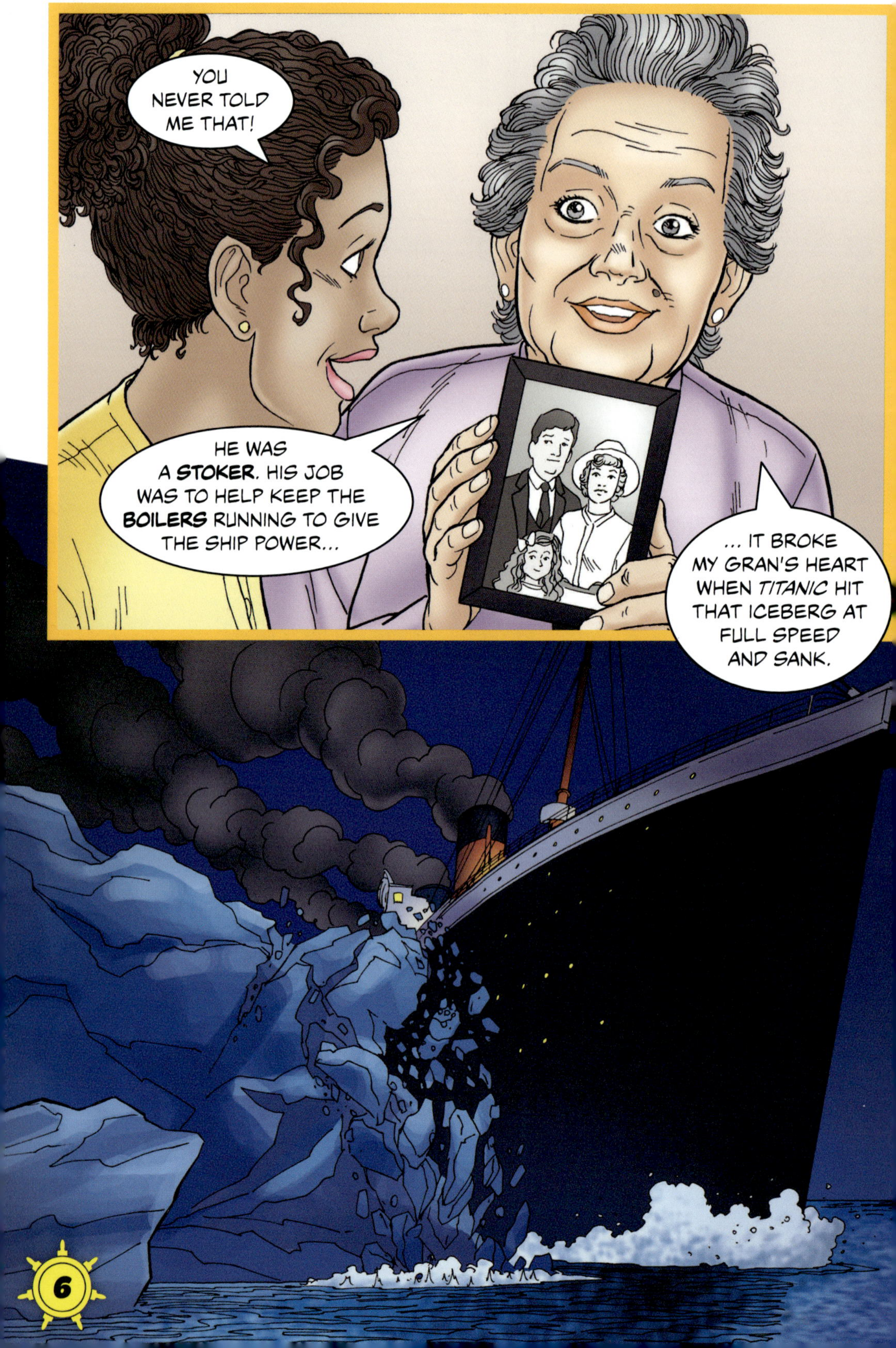
YOU NEVER TOLD ME THAT!
HE WAS A **STOKER**. HIS JOB WAS TO HELP KEEP THE **BOILERS** RUNNING TO GIVE THE SHIP POWER...
... IT BROKE MY GRAN'S HEART WHEN *TITANIC* HIT THAT ICEBERG AT FULL SPEED AND SANK.

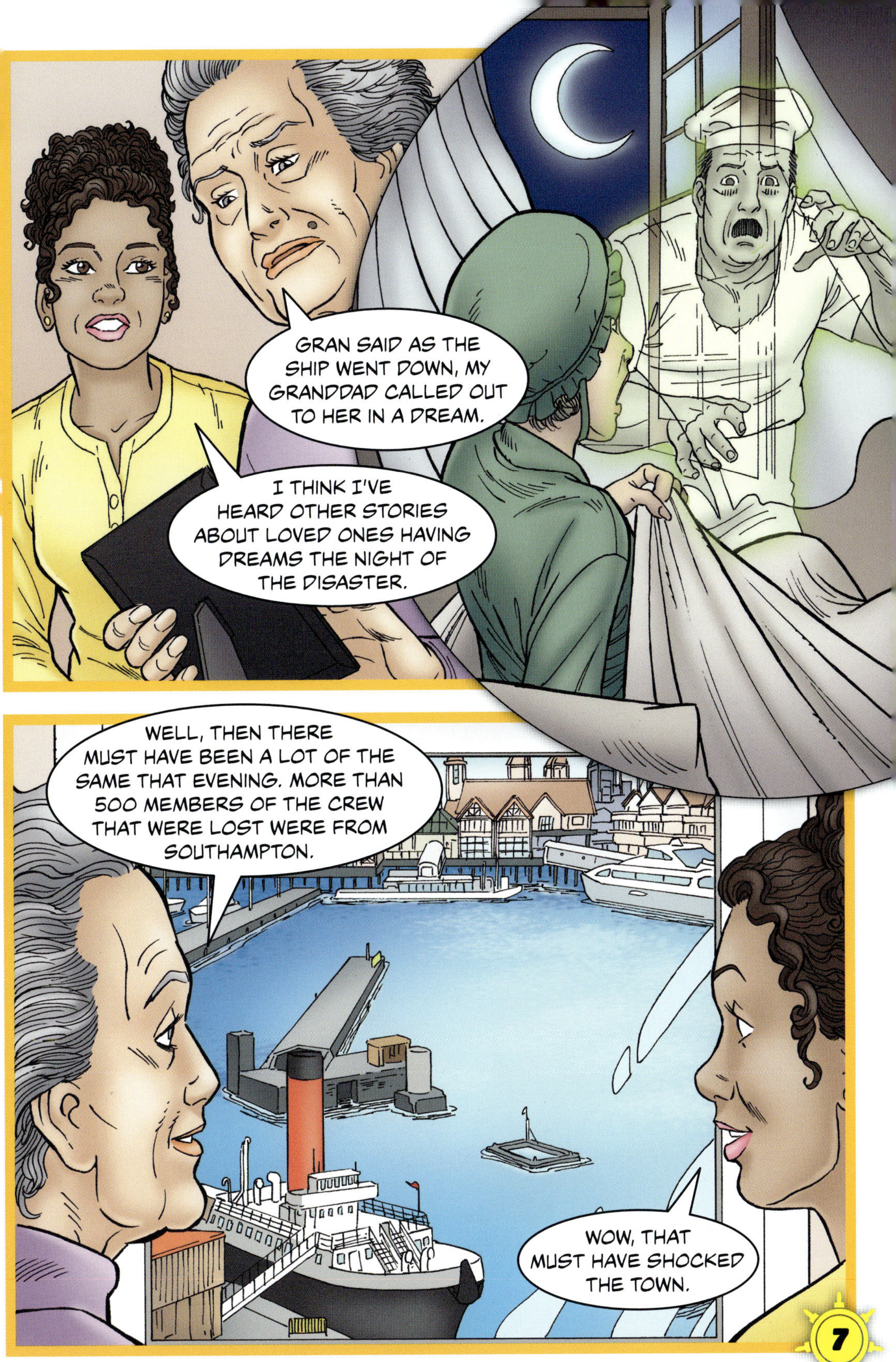
GRAN SAID AS THE SHIP WENT DOWN, MY GRANDDAD CALLED OUT TO HER IN A DREAM.
I THINK I'VE HEARD OTHER STORIES ABOUT LOVED ONES HAVING DREAMS THE NIGHT OF THE DISASTER.
WELL, THEN THERE MUST HAVE BEEN A LOT OF THE SAME THAT EVENING. MORE THAN 500 MEMBERS OF THE CREW THAT WERE LOST WERE FROM SOUTHAMPTON.
WOW, THAT MUST HAVE SHOCKED THE TOWN.

CHAPTER 2

A Big Idea

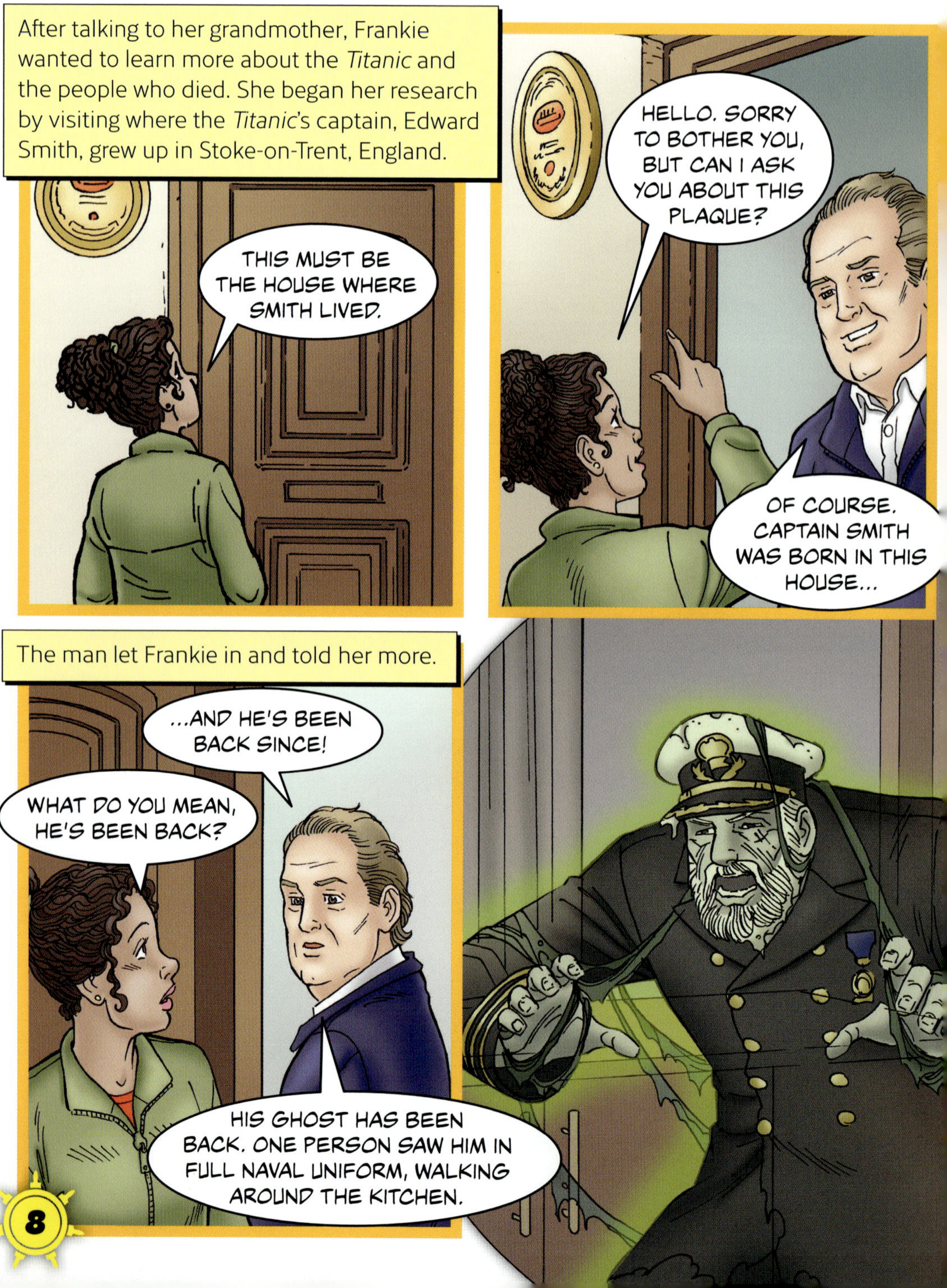
After talking to her grandmother, Frankie wanted to learn more about the *Titanic* and the people who died. She began her research by visiting where the *Titanic*'s captain, Edward Smith, grew up in Stoke-on-Trent, England.
THIS MUST BE THE HOUSE WHERE SMITH LIVED.
HELLO. SORRY TO BOTHER YOU, BUT CAN I ASK YOU ABOUT THIS PLAQUE?
OF COURSE. CAPTAIN SMITH WAS BORN IN THIS HOUSE...
The man let Frankie in and told her more.
...AND HE'S BEEN BACK SINCE!
WHAT DO YOU MEAN, HE'S BEEN BACK?
HIS GHOST HAS BEEN BACK. ONE PERSON SAW HIM IN FULL NAVAL UNIFORM, WALKING AROUND THE KITCHEN.

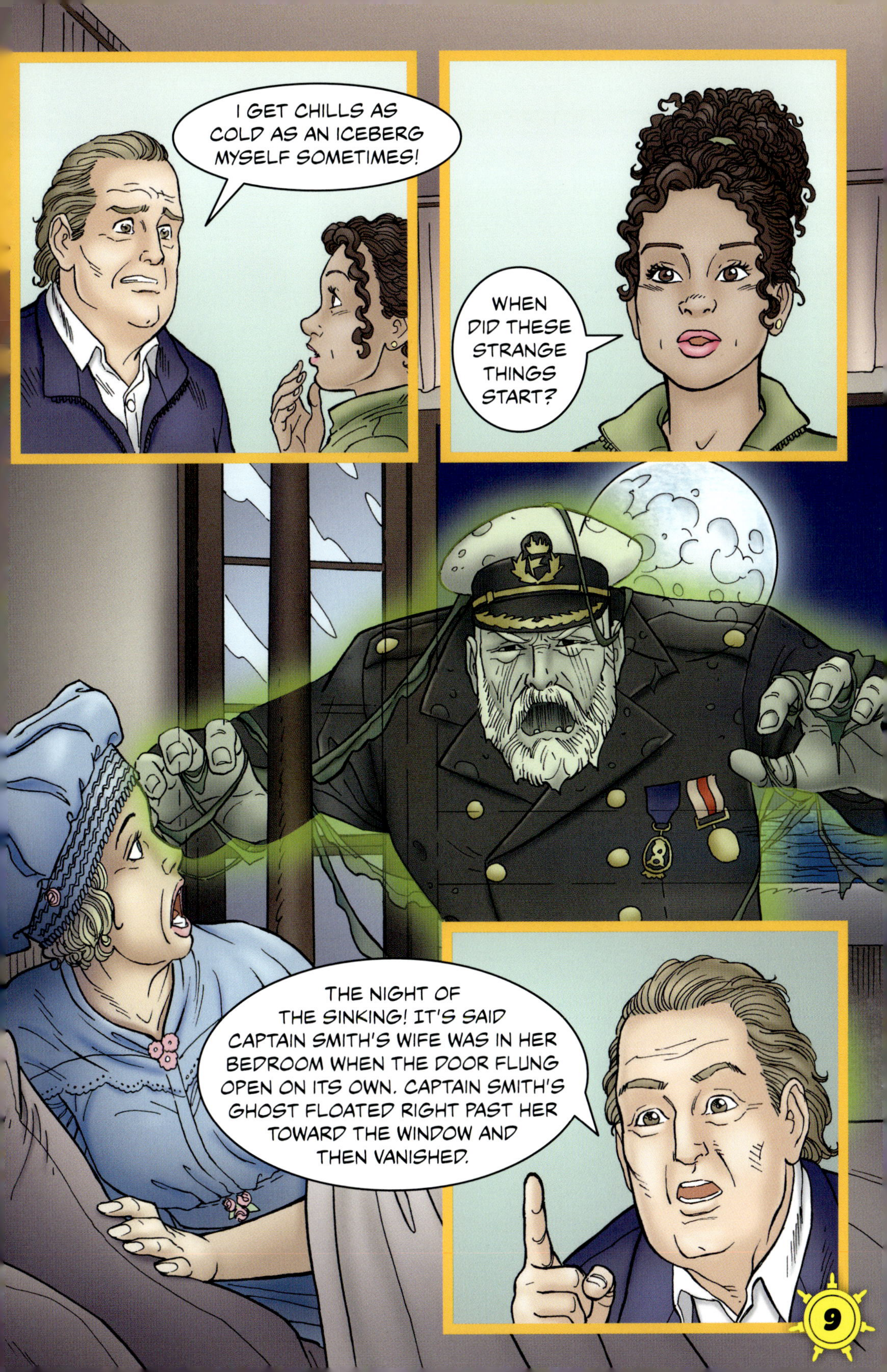
I GET CHILLS AS COLD AS AN ICEBERG MYSELF SOMETIMES!
WHEN DID THESE STRANGE THINGS START?
THE NIGHT OF THE SINKING! IT'S SAID CAPTAIN SMITH'S WIFE WAS IN HER BEDROOM WHEN THE DOOR FLUNG OPEN ON ITS OWN. CAPTAIN SMITH'S GHOST FLOATED RIGHT PAST HER TOWARD THE WINDOW AND THEN VANISHED.

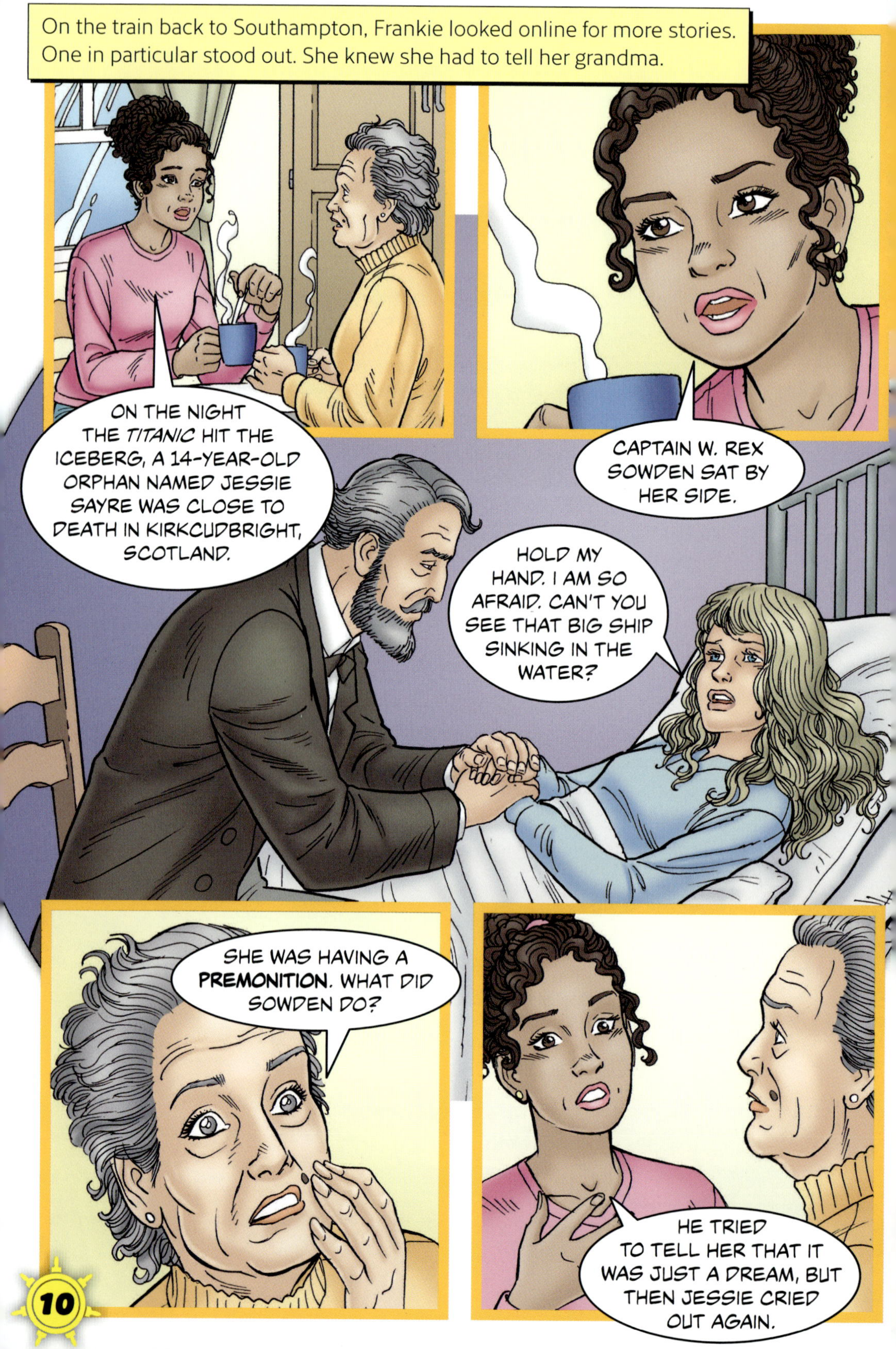
On the train back to Southampton, Frankie looked online for more stories. One in particular stood out. She knew she had to tell her grandma.
ON THE NIGHT THE *TITANIC* HIT THE ICEBERG, A 14-YEAR-OLD ORPHAN NAMED JESSIE SAYRE WAS CLOSE TO DEATH IN KIRKCUDBRIGHT, SCOTLAND.
CAPTAIN W. REX SOWDEN SAT BY HER SIDE.
HOLD MY HAND. I AM SO AFRAID. CAN'T YOU SEE THAT BIG SHIP SINKING IN THE WATER?
SHE WAS HAVING A **PREMONITION**. WHAT DID SOWDEN DO?
HE TRIED TO TELL HER THAT IT WAS JUST A DREAM, BUT THEN JESSIE CRIED OUT AGAIN.

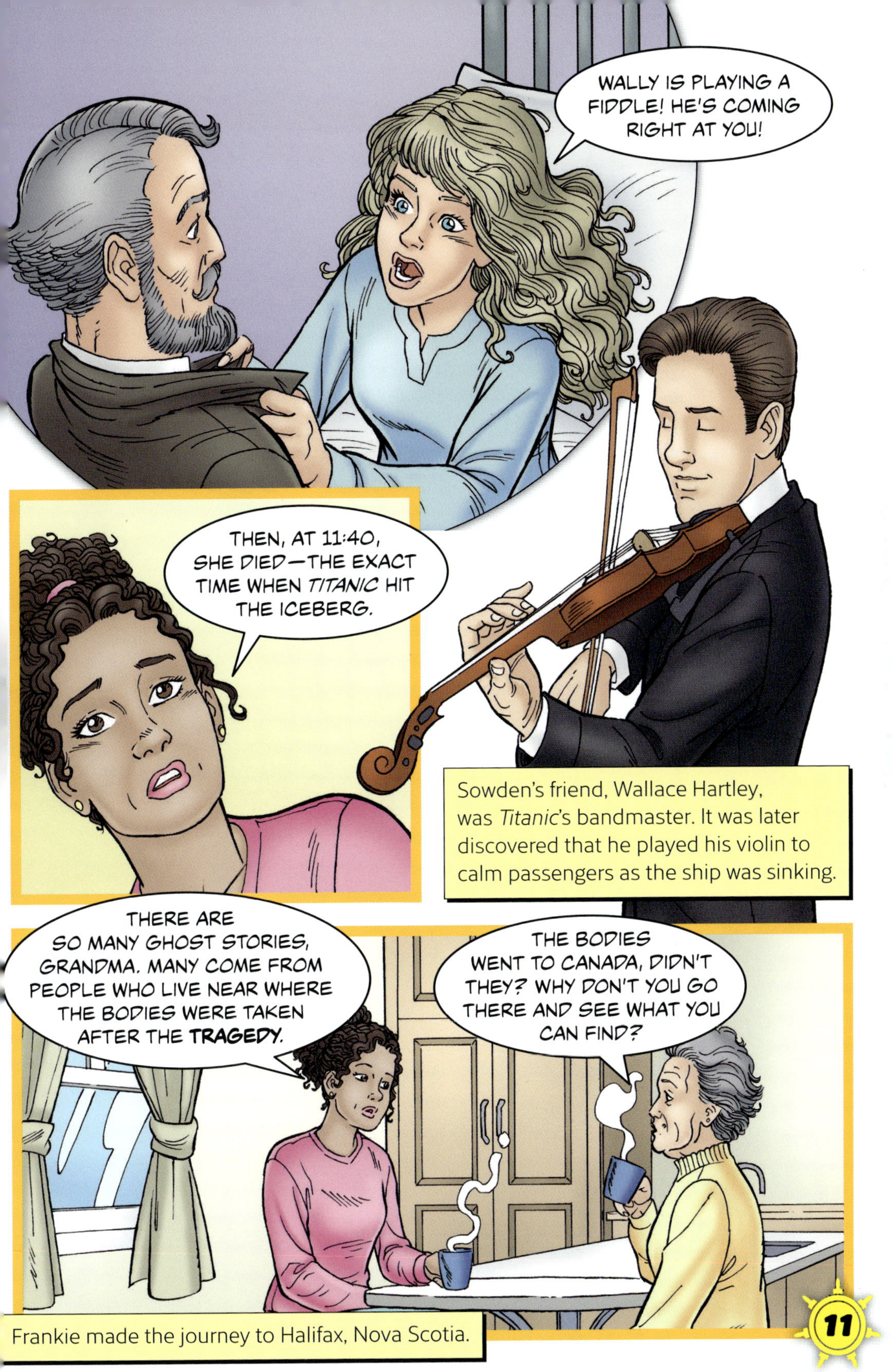

WALLY IS PLAYING A FIDDLE! HE'S COMING RIGHT AT YOU!
THEN, AT 11:40, SHE DIED—THE EXACT TIME WHEN *TITANIC* HIT THE ICEBERG.
Sowden's friend, Wallace Hartley, was *Titanic*'s bandmaster. It was later discovered that he played his violin to calm passengers as the ship was sinking.
THERE ARE SO MANY GHOST STORIES, GRANDMA. MANY COME FROM PEOPLE WHO LIVE NEAR WHERE THE BODIES WERE TAKEN AFTER THE **TRAGEDY**.
THE BODIES WENT TO CANADA, DIDN'T THEY? WHY DON'T YOU GO THERE AND SEE WHAT YOU CAN FIND?
Frankie made the journey to Halifax, Nova Scotia.

CHAPTER 3

Ghostly Restaurant

In Nova Scotia, Frankie visited the Five Fishermen restaurant, where she spoke with the owner.

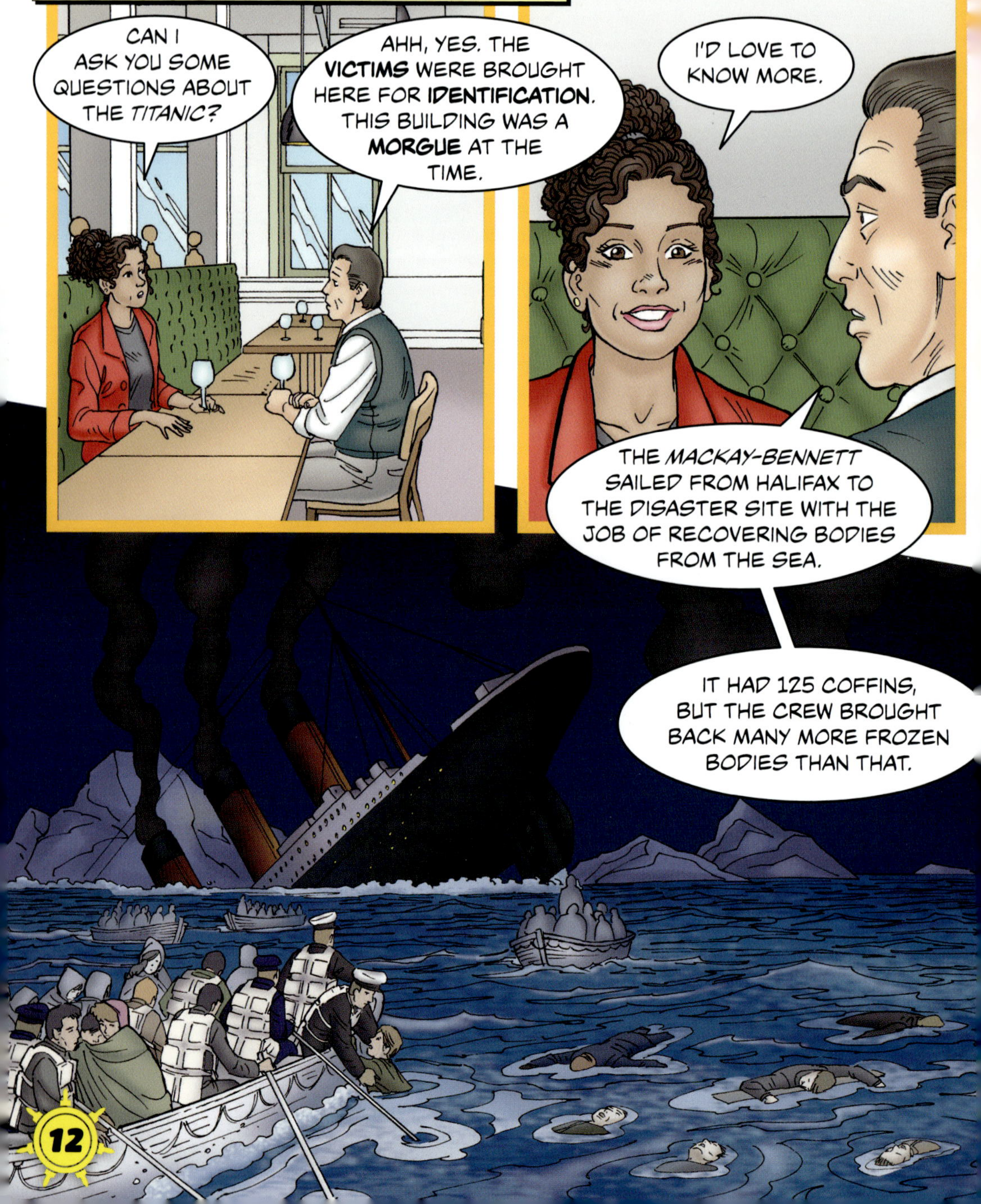

CAN I ASK YOU SOME QUESTIONS ABOUT THE *TITANIC*?
AHH, YES. THE **VICTIMS** WERE BROUGHT HERE FOR **IDENTIFICATION**. THIS BUILDING WAS A **MORGUE** AT THE TIME.
I'D LOVE TO KNOW MORE.
THE *MACKAY-BENNETT* SAILED FROM HALIFAX TO THE DISASTER SITE WITH THE JOB OF RECOVERING BODIES FROM THE SEA.
IT HAD 125 COFFINS, BUT THE CREW BROUGHT BACK MANY MORE FROZEN BODIES THAN THAT.

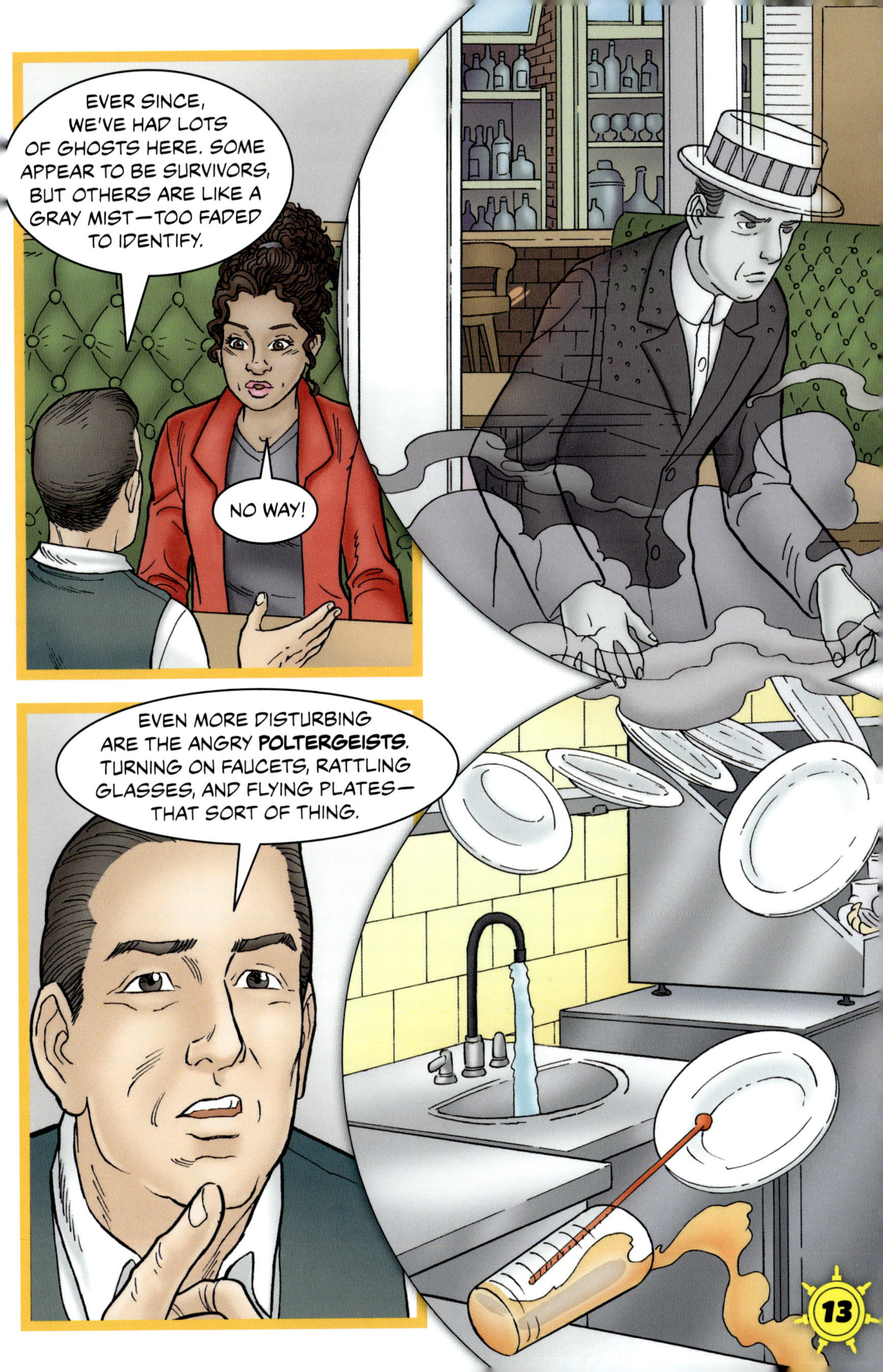
EVER SINCE, WE'VE HAD LOTS OF GHOSTS HERE. SOME APPEAR TO BE SURVIVORS, BUT OTHERS ARE LIKE A GRAY MIST—TOO FADED TO IDENTIFY.
NO WAY!
EVEN MORE DISTURBING ARE THE ANGRY **POLTERGEISTS**. TURNING ON FAUCETS, RATTLING GLASSES, AND FLYING PLATES—THAT SORT OF THING.

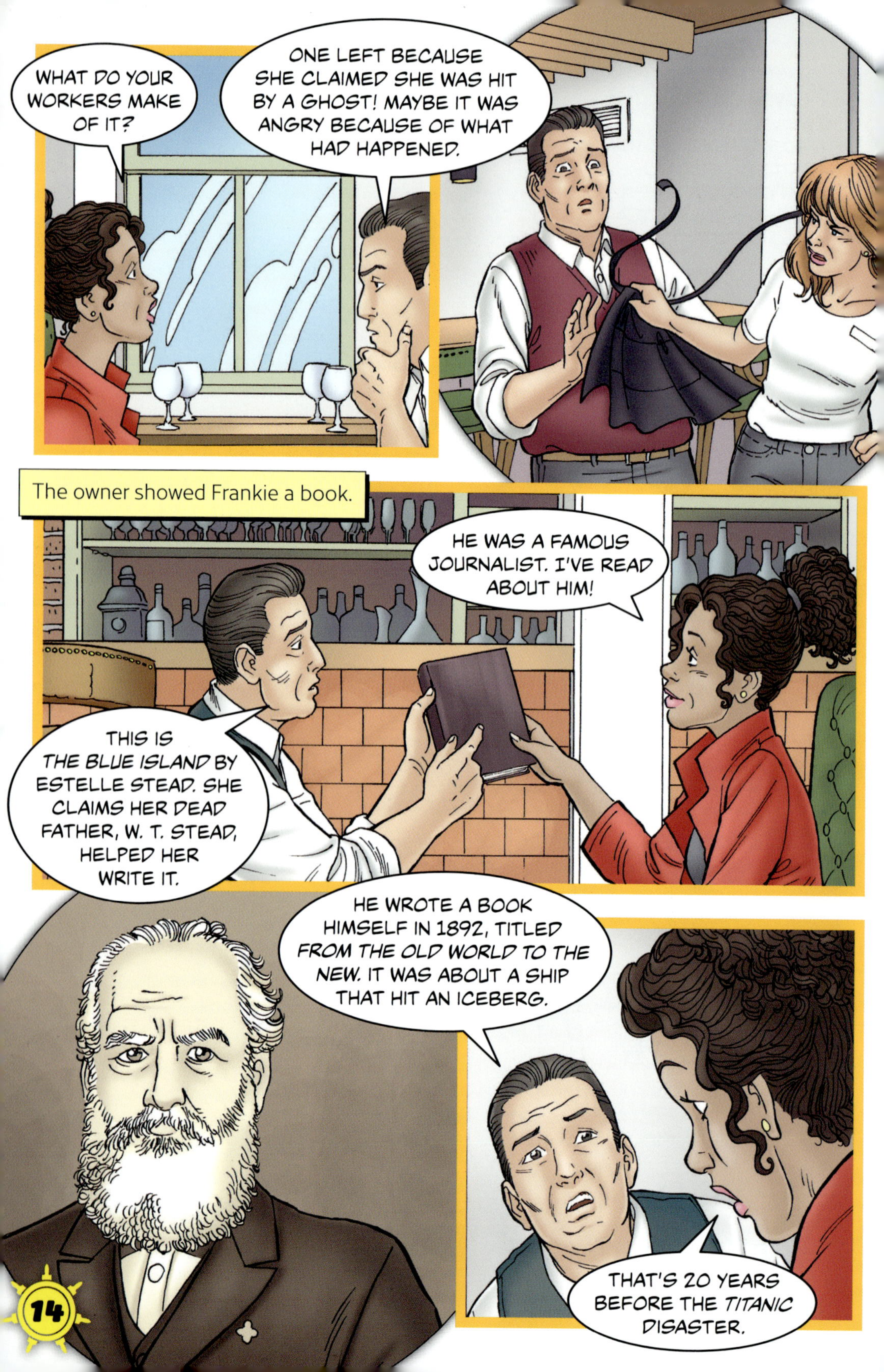
WHAT DO YOUR WORKERS MAKE OF IT?
ONE LEFT BECAUSE SHE CLAIMED SHE WAS HIT BY A GHOST! MAYBE IT WAS ANGRY BECAUSE OF WHAT HAD HAPPENED.
The owner showed Frankie a book.
HE WAS A FAMOUS JOURNALIST. I'VE READ ABOUT HIM!
THIS IS *THE BLUE ISLAND* BY ESTELLE STEAD. SHE CLAIMS HER DEAD FATHER, W. T. STEAD, HELPED HER WRITE IT.
HE WROTE A BOOK HIMSELF IN 1892, TITLED *FROM THE OLD WORLD TO THE NEW*. IT WAS ABOUT A SHIP THAT HIT AN ICEBERG.
THAT'S 20 YEARS BEFORE THE *TITANIC* DISASTER.

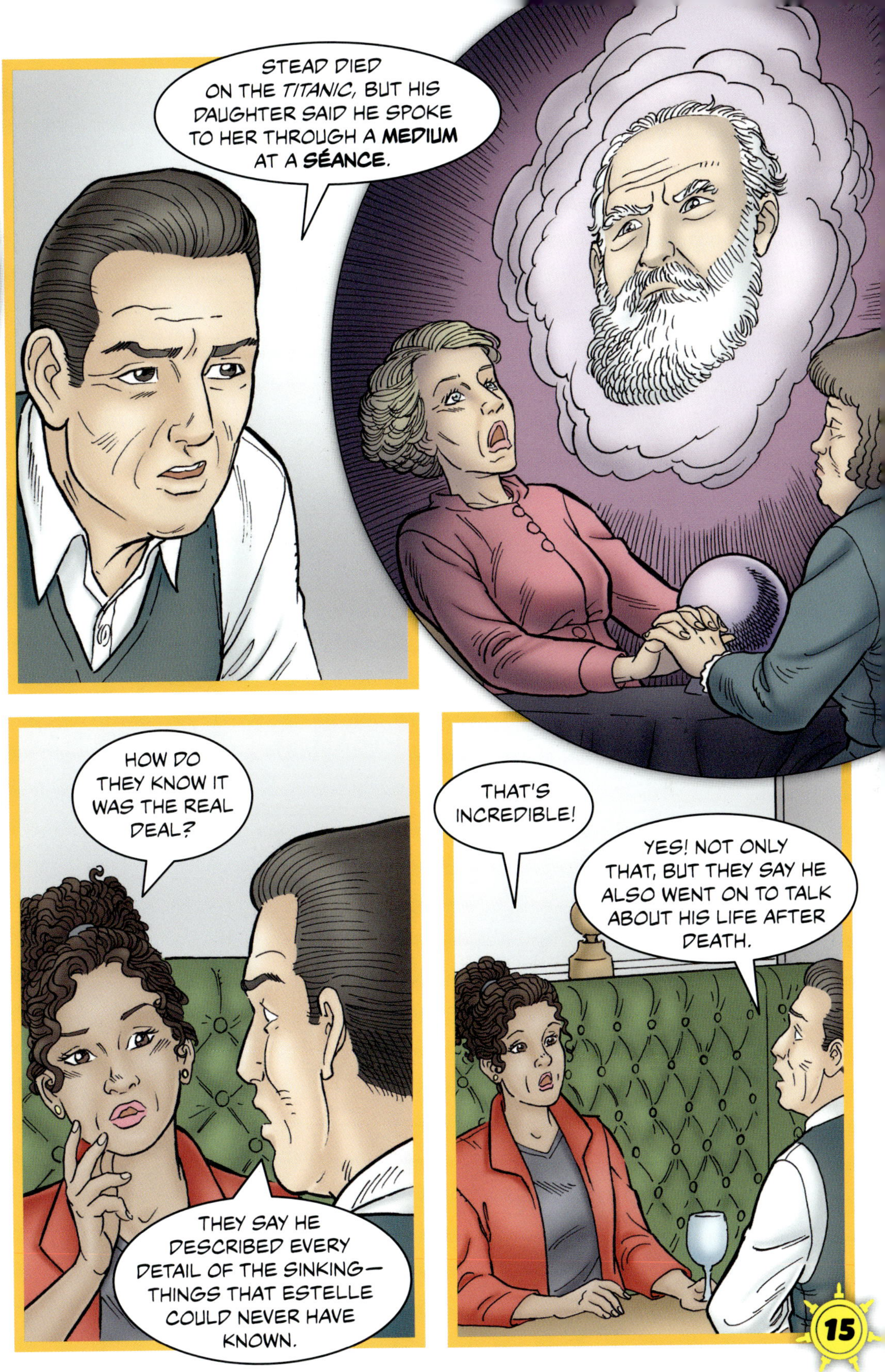
STEAD DIED ON THE *TITANIC*, BUT HIS DAUGHTER SAID HE SPOKE TO HER THROUGH A **MEDIUM** AT A **SÉANCE**.
HOW DO THEY KNOW IT WAS THE REAL DEAL?
THEY SAY HE DESCRIBED EVERY DETAIL OF THE SINKING— THINGS THAT ESTELLE COULD NEVER HAVE KNOWN.
THAT'S INCREDIBLE!
YES! NOT ONLY THAT, BUT THEY SAY HE ALSO WENT ON TO TALK ABOUT HIS LIFE AFTER DEATH.

CHAPTER 4

Eerie Exhibits

Next, Frankie headed to the Maritime Museum of the Atlantic in Halifax. There, she viewed many **artifacts** from *Titanic*.

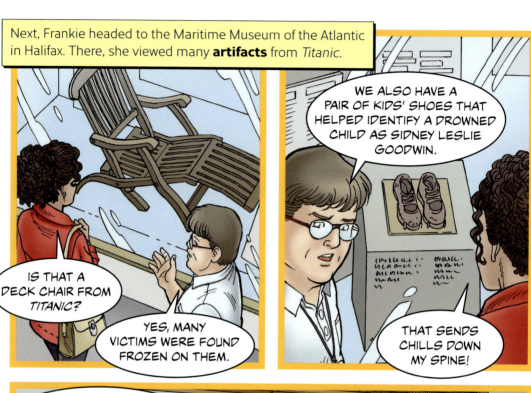

IS THAT A DECK CHAIR FROM *TITANIC*?

YES, MANY VICTIMS WERE FOUND FROZEN ON THEM.

WE ALSO HAVE A PAIR OF KIDS' SHOES THAT HELPED IDENTIFY A DROWNED CHILD AS SIDNEY LESLIE GOODWIN.

THAT SENDS CHILLS DOWN MY SPINE!

JUST BE GRATEFUL YOU DON'T HAVE TO RELIVE THE SINKING.

WHAT DO YOU MEAN?

WE'VE HAD GHOSTS! PARANORMAL INVESTIGATORS ONCE RECORDED A GHOSTLY VOICE AT THE EXHIBIT.

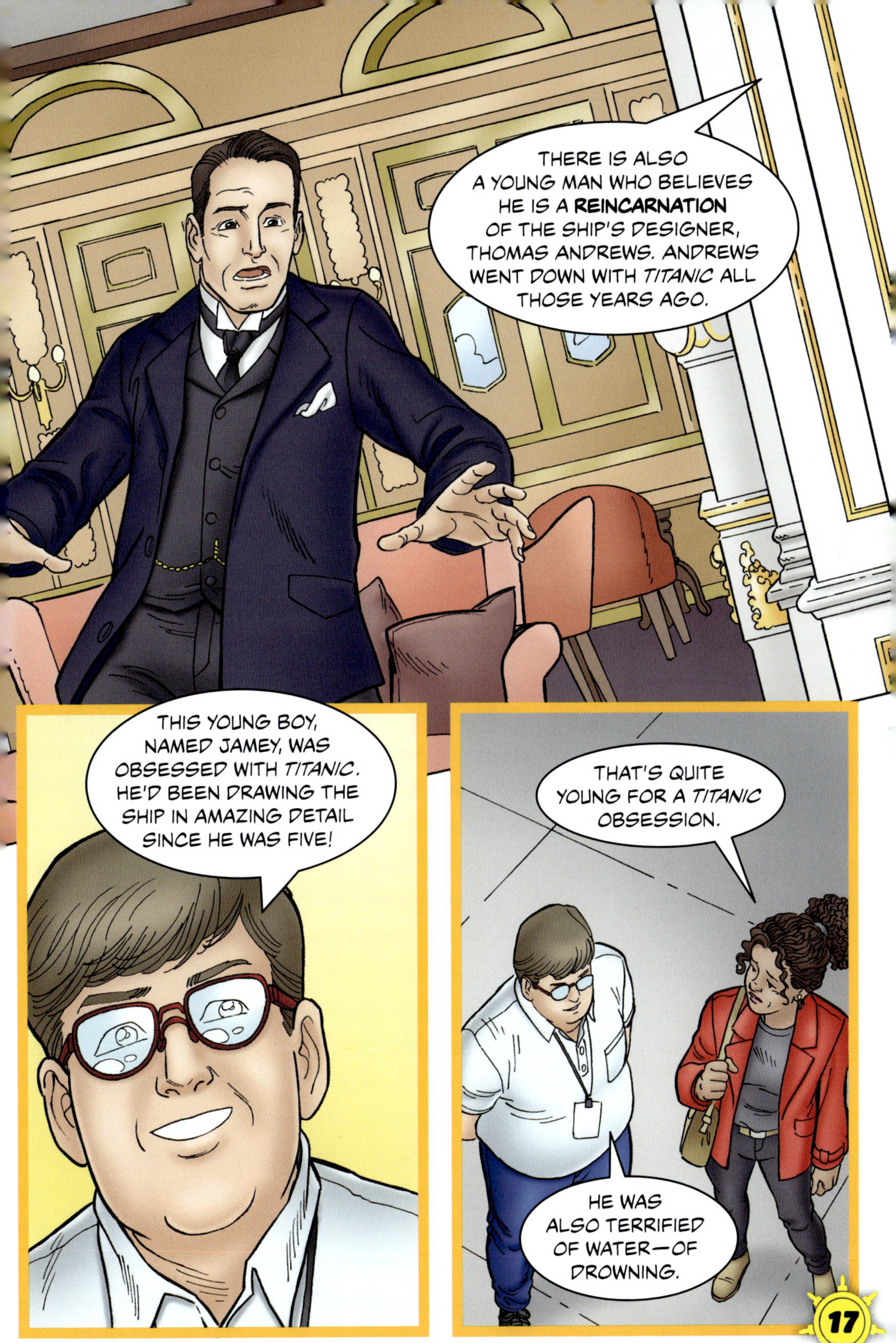
THERE IS ALSO A YOUNG MAN WHO BELIEVES HE IS A **REINCARNATION** OF THE SHIP'S DESIGNER, THOMAS ANDREWS. ANDREWS WENT DOWN WITH *TITANIC* ALL THOSE YEARS AGO.
THIS YOUNG BOY, NAMED JAMEY, WAS OBSESSED WITH *TITANIC*. HE'D BEEN DRAWING THE SHIP IN AMAZING DETAIL SINCE HE WAS FIVE!
THAT'S QUITE YOUNG FOR A *TITANIC* OBSESSION.
HE WAS ALSO TERRIFIED OF WATER—OF DROWNING.

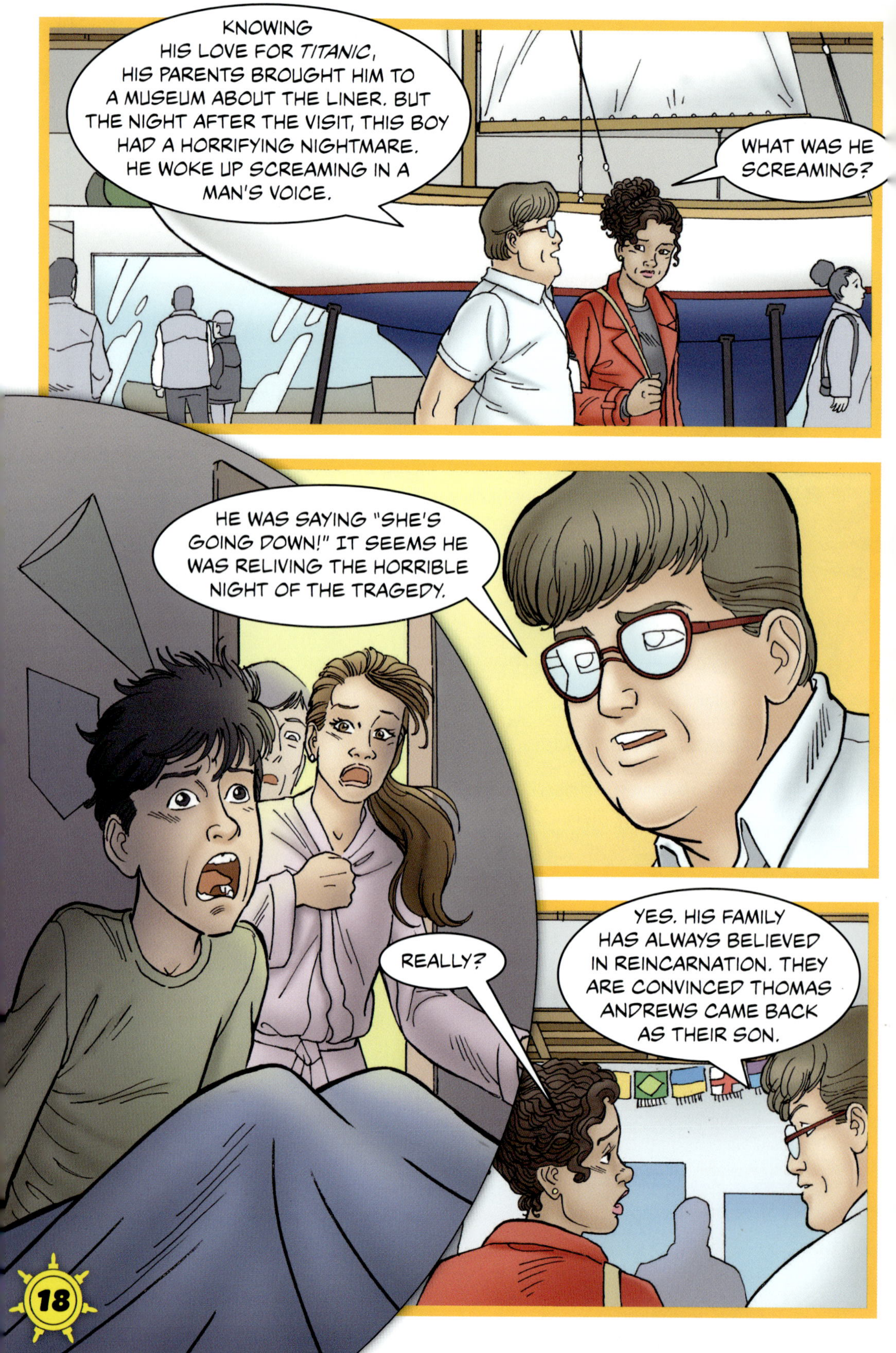
KNOWING HIS LOVE FOR *TITANIC*, HIS PARENTS BROUGHT HIM TO A MUSEUM ABOUT THE LINER. BUT THE NIGHT AFTER THE VISIT, THIS BOY HAD A HORRIFYING NIGHTMARE. HE WOKE UP SCREAMING IN A MAN'S VOICE.
WHAT WAS HE SCREAMING?
HE WAS SAYING "SHE'S GOING DOWN!" IT SEEMS HE WAS RELIVING THE HORRIBLE NIGHT OF THE TRAGEDY.
REALLY?
YES. HIS FAMILY HAS ALWAYS BELIEVED IN REINCARNATION. THEY ARE CONVINCED THOMAS ANDREWS CAME BACK AS THEIR SON.

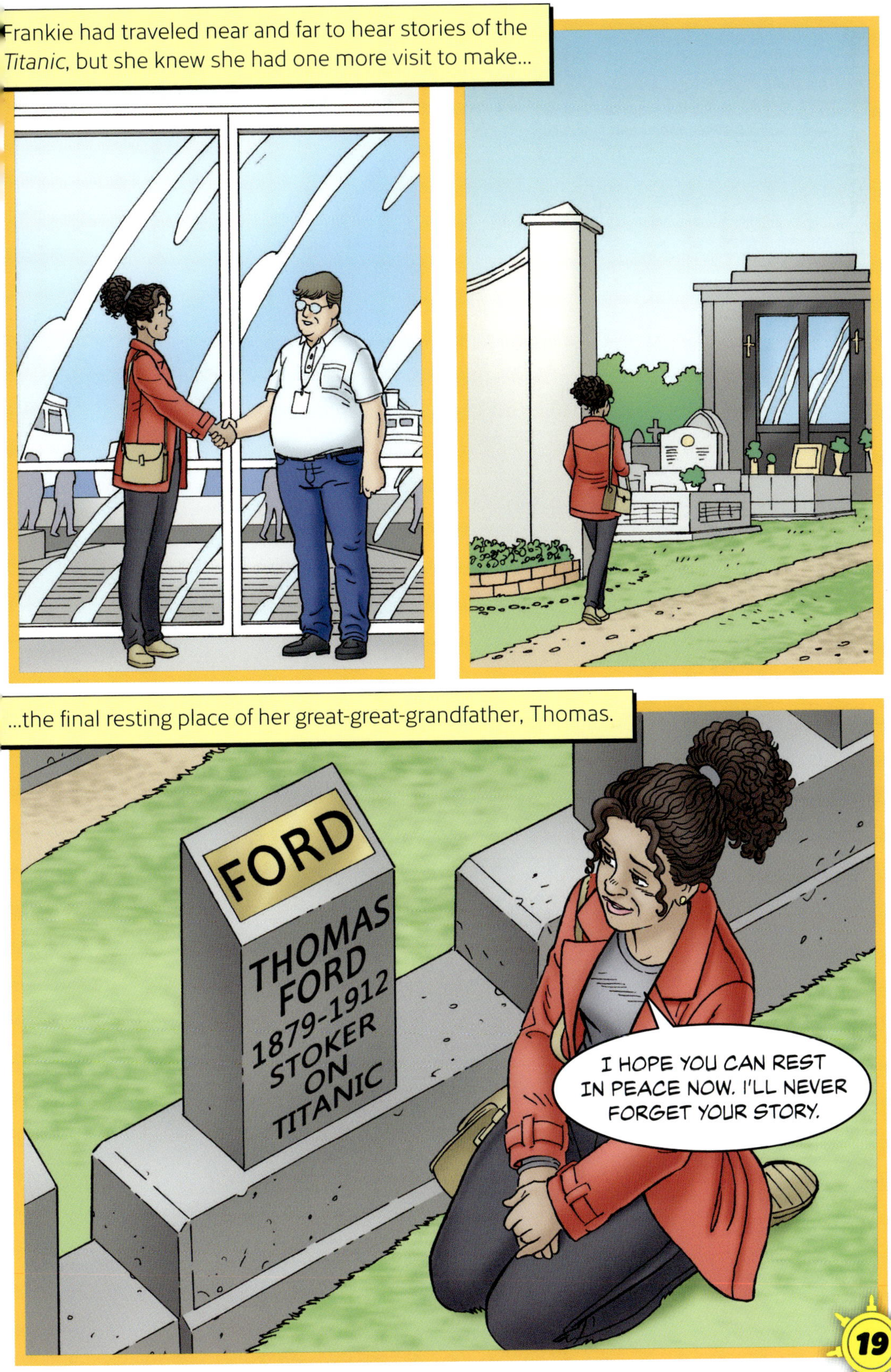
Frankie had traveled near and far to hear stories of the *Titanic*, but she knew she had one more visit to make...
...the final resting place of her great-great-grandfather, Thomas.
FORD
THOMAS FORD 1879-1912 STOKER ON TITANIC
I HOPE YOU CAN REST IN PEACE NOW. I'LL NEVER FORGET YOUR STORY.

Visits from a Watery Grave

The ghost of Captain Edward Smith has been seen many times. He's been spotted in his old childhood home, in a pub in Ireland, and in a hotel suite in Liverpool. On the anniversary of the sinking, Smith is said to appear in a mirror he left on his dressing table before he set sail on *Titanic*.

Visitors and staff at *Titanic* exhibitions have also reported strange things—the strong feeling of being watched or followed; hearing voices, footsteps, and music; and seeing eerie lights or shadowy figures. A cleaner at an exhibition in Orlando, Florida, said she saw a gentleman in a top hat sitting in one of the *Titanic* deck chairs on display. In another exhibition, a young woman in a black old-fashioned dress is said to walk down the grand staircase.

ONE OF THE SURVIVING DECK CHAIRS FROM *TITANIC*

Artifacts from the disaster include top hats, shoes, and stopped watches. When one of the ship's musician's body was recovered from the Atlantic, his violin case was strapped to his back and sheet music was found in a leather case beneath his life jacket. Ships passing over the **wreck** site have reported hearing an orchestra playing, as well as the sounds of people shouting for help.

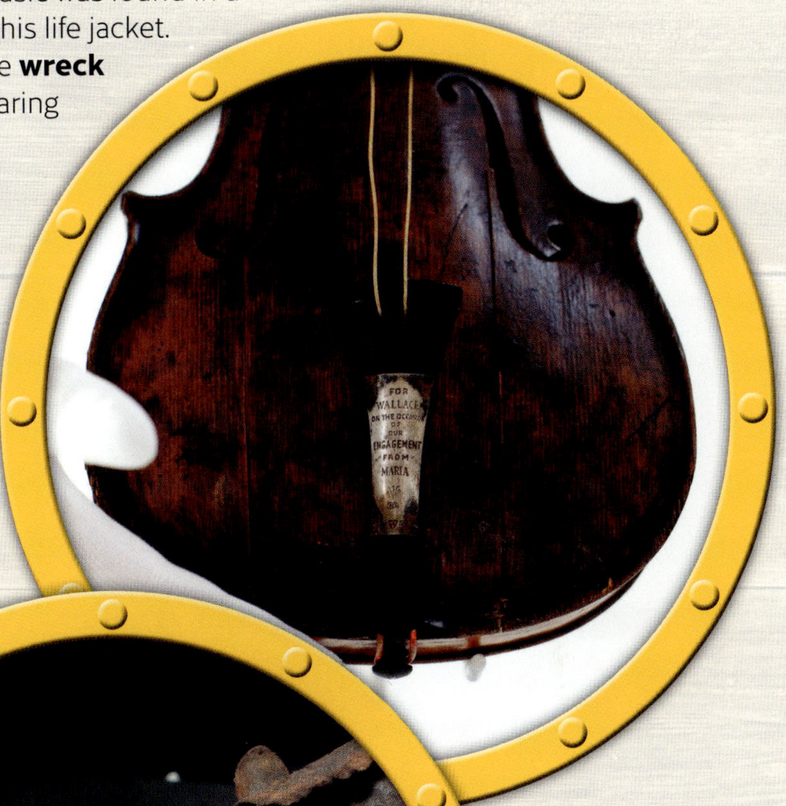
FOR
WALLACE
OF
OUR
ENGAGEMENT
FROM
MARIA

WALLACE HARTLEY'S VIOLIN

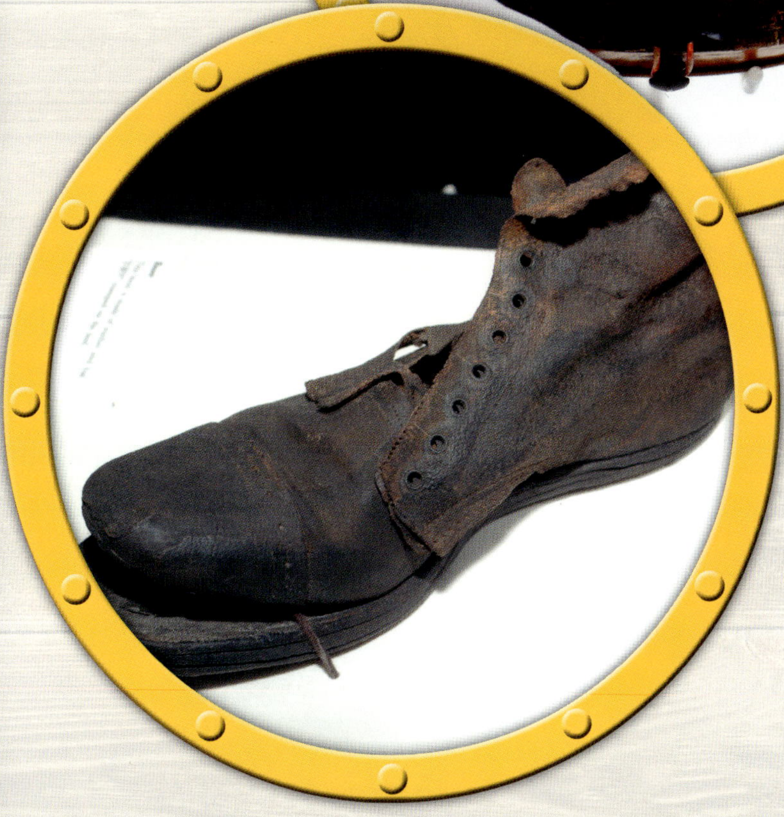

A SHOE—ONE OF THE MANY ARTIFACTS FROM A PASSENGER ON THE *TITANIC*

More Titanic Stories

Titanic's musicians were expected to play any tune a passenger requested. When disaster struck, the musicians were asked to play to keep everyone calm. Although they were technically members of the crew, they were also considered second-class passengers. They could have chosen to save themselves as the boat went down. Instead, they stayed on the sinking ship, playing for more than two hours. Without music stands and in poor light, the musicians played pieces they all knew from memory. When the ship went down, all of the men sank with it.

TITANIC'S MUSICIANS

THE JANE HOTEL

After the *Titanic* disaster, many surviving members of the crew were taken to a boarding house in New York City. It was built by the American Seamen's Friend Society (ASFS), a religious organization working to improve the welfare of seamen in the United States and abroad. Today, this building is the Jane Hotel and is said to be haunted by some of these survivors. Occasionally, the elevator goes up or down by itself, visitors have spotted shadowy figures, and the halls are sometimes filled with sounds of sobbing.

Glossary

artifacts human-made objects

boilers parts of an engine that make steam to produce power

identification the process of figuring out who or what something is

medium a person said to be able to communicate with dead people

morgue a room where dead bodies are kept

ocean liners large ships that can carry many people across the ocean

poltergeists ghosts or spirits thought to be able to make loud noises and move objects

premonition a strong feeling that something is about to happen

reincarnation being reborn in another body

séance an event at which a medium communicates with a dead person

stoker a person who tends a furnace on a steamship

tragedy a terrible event

victims people who are harmed, injured, or killed as the result of a crime or accident

wreck the remains of a ship that was destroyed at sea

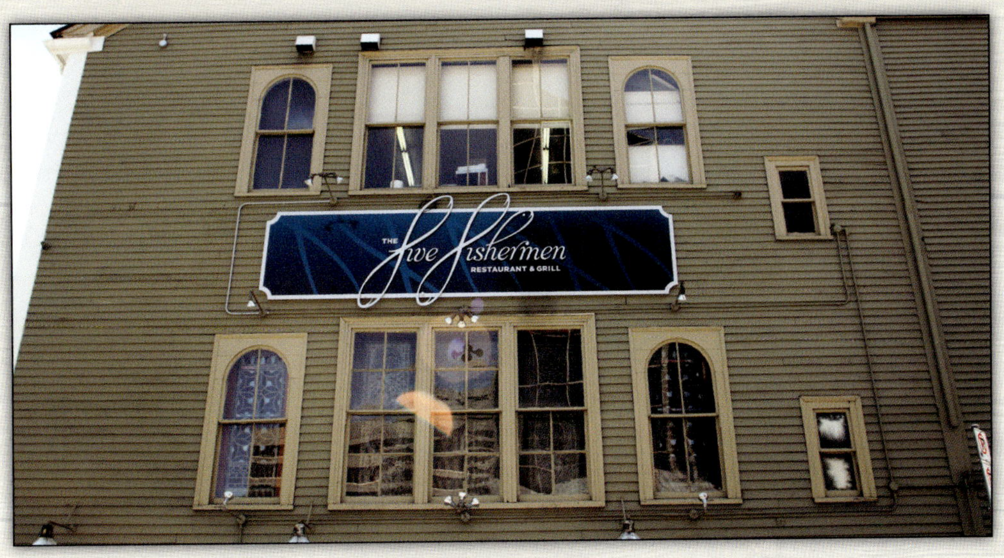
THE
Five Fishermen
RESTAURANT & GRILL

THE FIVE FISHERMEN RESTAURANT WAS A FUNERAL HOME IN 1912 WHEN IT SERVED AS A MORGUE FOR THE BODIES RECOVERED FROM THE *TITANIC* SINKING.

Index

Read More

Andrews, Elizabeth. *Haunted Ships (Hauntings)*.
Minneapolis: Pop!, 2022.

Eason, Sarah. *Disaster Strikes! (Tragedy! Tales from the* Titanic*)*.
Minneapolis: Bearport Publishing Company, 2025.

Parkin, Michelle. *Atlantic Ocean Shipwrecks (Famous Shipwrecks)*.
Minneapolis: Jump, Inc., 2024.

Learn More Online

1. Go to **FactSurfer.com** or scan the QR code below.
2. Enter "**Haunted Titanic Stories**" into the search box.
3. Click on the cover of this book to see a list of websites.